# DICISION MAKING

I0468811

## *HOW TO MAKE THE RIGHT DICISION EVERY TIME*

## BY BEVERLY HILL

# Introduction

I want to thank you and congratulate you for choosing the book, *"DECISION MAKING: HOW TO MAKE THE RIGHT DECISION EVERY TIME"*.

This book contains proven steps and strategies on how to become a better decision maker, and reach the right decisions every time.

"Those who reach decisions promptly definitely know what they want and generally get it. The leaders in every walk of life decide quickly and firmly. That is the major reason why they are leaders. The world has the habit of making room for people whose words and actions show." *Napoleon Hill*

Decision is a single mental action that has the power to change any personal problem. The certain decisions have the potential to provide you an immense success. All the people who learned, and mastered decision making are very successful in everything they do. They differ from others because they are capable of changing the circumstances around them within a very short amount of time, just because they make the right decision at the right time.

Decision making is not just important in your business, but also in every other area of your life. This force affects your whole life, your relationships, family, social life, and also physical and mental health. Like any other mental ability, you can also develop your ability of decision making. You have to do it by yourself, through unwavering discipline, and proper understanding of the power of this force.

The best way is to learn to listen to your gut feelings, your inner voice that knowing place inside you that is called your intuition. In many cases, our parents taught us to rationalize, to think and analyze all the facts then crunch the numbers and make a decision. Sometimes that works, but if you talk to highly successful people, they all rely to some degree on their intuition. They seem to know when it is time to go by the book, or go with the flow. Flow has more fluidity and has more flexibility to move, change, and morph into the best of the best. Our natural innate energy exchanges blend with other energies to become the best idea, the best solution, or the best something. When rules and limitations come into play, the flow is restricted. Limitations and excuses try to sneak their way into the decision.

By allowing your intuition to blossom and interact with the flow, the flow increases and widens, providing even more opportunities. The natural rhythm and order of things becomes more synchronous, and the decision seems to emerge rather than having to be wrestled with. New inspiration is birthed, and more and more energy pours into the flow. You seem to know exactly what to do, and when to do it. Decisions become more of an art than an agony. As you listen to that inner you, you are automatically steered in the right direction. It's like you've got this eagle, high up in the sky, telling you what is ahead so you can move in the right direction, and be ready when it get here.

Thanks again for choosing this book, I hope you enjoy it!

# ABOUT THE AUTHOR

Beverly Hill is a sociologist. She is the CEO of C.E.F Associates and formerly served as head of department of sociology in Premier Natural Resources Inc.

A graduate of Nelson High School also graduated from the University of Toronto with a B.A in economics and finance and holds an M.S from Cambridge University in public relations and PhD in sociology.

She has written many articles on human equality, animal rights, environmental issues, personal development and peace keeping in different newspapers. She has also appeared in many magazines and is frequently interviewed for articles on family, race, socioeconomic status, and how to survive in your environment. She has also worked on the importance of health of relationship between parents and children. Her book 'The Middle Child' focuses on the importance of the attention given to the children and what to expect from them. This book helps parents understand their children.

In addition to these works she is also the author of 'Surviving Alone ' which is about her own childhood growing up; she writes about her family struggles living on a low income budget and growing her own food to survive.

C.E.F Associates formed in 1999 in Idaho, USA she worked both nationally and internationally. This is a consulting company which has clients all over the world. Ms. Hill the

CEO of the company is the main reason of the huge client base because of her servings in foreign countries.

# TABLE OF CONTENT

# Chapter 1

## METHODS OF DECISION MAKING

Have you notice how many decision you have to make every day? From the moment you get up you are bombarded by decisions demanding your attention. Will I wear the blue shirt of white? Will I walk to work or drive? What will I buy for lunch or dinner?

Most of these decisions are easy enough to make and you know that your life won't hang in the balance if you make the wrong call. But there are other decisions which are far more difficult because there is a lot riding on them.

There are many methods of decision-making. One of the most often used is the Pros and Cons approach. You write a list of reasons why you should do something, and another list for why you shouldn't. The list that is the longest/strongest is what you do. But people who use this technique often feel uncomfortable when they've made a decision this way. Why? Because this is a logical or rational approach to decision-making, and many of us don't have logic as our strongest sense.'

What I mean by this is that just like some of us are visual learners and others are auditory learners, some of us have more effective methods of making decisions than logic. Logic is just one method. It's not the only method. And I am going to go out on a limb here, and say it may not even be the best method for many people just because it's the logical choice don't make it the right choice. Only time will tell about that. So how do you know what method is best for you? If you are a pragmatic, down to earthy type you are better going with what has worked in the past, or something that seems the practical solution.

If you're an emotional person, then go with what feels right to you. You can imagine the situation, and then do an emotional inventory. How does it feel to go down this path? If it feels good, do it, if it doesn't –find another path.

If you're a fiery, impulsive type, then you are better off trusting your gut-your intuition. Often your first decision is the right one for you.

And lastly, if you are an analytical person who trusts logic, then go with the pros and cons approach. Most of us don't totally fit into one of these boxes. But we will all have one or two that are stronger, and at least one that is weakest. The trick is to know what not to use. It's the least likely to net you the best results.

How do you know what your weakest one is? Think back to a time when you were very tired, and had to make a decision. What of the 4 methods outlined above did you use? This is likely to be your weakest, and the least effective method for you.

When I'm tired or stressed my mind goes around in circles, and I start making lists of pros and cons. It is definitely not my best method. When I'm powering on all cylinders, I just know what I need to do. I'm one of the fiery impulsive types. Over the years it's rarely led me wrong. But those pros and cons listed has more than once.

# Chapter 2

## DISCOVER HOW TO MAKE THE RIGHT CHOICE

Every day you are always asked to make decision: Should I go left or right? Should I do this or not? But making a decision is not what's really important. What matters is you choose the right one.

## BUT HOW DO YOU EXACTLY DO IT?

Making the right decision is highly essential. After all, the wrong one always carries consequences, some of which are so detrimental you don't want to experience them. Take for example, choosing the bus instead of the subway. It may turn out that the latter takes so much of your time, preventing you from coming to work early. In the process, you don't get a lot of tasks done at the end of the day, and you have to extend your working hours. You also miss out on an early dinner party with a friend.

Here are some tips that may help you come up with a right decision:

Know the pros and cons. Keep in mind the advantages and disadvantages of every decision that you're going to make. Don't be biased. Sometimes you've already formed an initial decision in your mind, so you either don't list all the cons or all the pros. The general guideline is the pros should out weight the cons, regardless of how many disadvantages you have listed. If after careful consideration, you realize that the pros are the things you really want, and you can handle the consequences, then you should go for that decision.

Learn from the past. You know what they say; if you commit the same mistake again, you're already a fool. Before you decide, go back to your past experiences. Have you met this type of crossroad before? What was your decision? If it failed, then you already know to take the other road.

However, it's not only your past that can matter. You can also learn from other people's experiences. If you are having a hard time making the correct decision, look for someone who has gone past it. Ask him or her what he or she did, and if he or she was successful or not. Remind yourself to make the right one. There are times when you're biased over a certain decision. Even if you know that it's wrong, or it involves a lot of risks, you have the great desire to go for it. But before you do that remind yourself first of your main goal.

Use affirmations or subliminal messages to tell yourself that there's a need for you to make the right move. You can say, "I choose decisions that would make me a better person", or "I pick decisions that have the least ill consequences to me and to others", You have to say the latter as decisions can affect not only you but also your loved ones.

Subliminal messages can also be used when you're visualizing or meditating. These two are also helpful in the discernment process, as they give you a clearer picture of what to do to reach your goals.

# Chapter 3

## DO YOU KNOW HOW TO MAKE THE RIGHT DECISION?

Making decisions is part of modern life, and each day we make hundreds of simple decisions, a handful of important decision, and occasionally, a missive decision. The problem is often in knowing the right or best thing to do, and so many of us do not know how to set about making the right decision.

## TAKE CARE WITH YOUR DECISIONS

You may be a student, and on whim decide for or against continuing your studies; little do you realize that a simple decision taken on a sunny afternoon on the playing fields of youth can decide whether you get a promotion, and salary raise on the battle fields of adult life, some 15-years later. You may be ten years into your career, and find you are overlooked for a plum job in a new division; you get drunk that night, and decide whether to remain in that occupation, or seek a new challenge with another company. You may be an athlete, or budding sports personality as a youth, and at your first setback, or when the training starts to bite hard, you wonder whether to quit.

The one thing you do not realize at that time, and do not take it into consideration, is that the waves from your decision will continue to spread out and touch lives, for the rest of time. If Fidel Castro had realized his athletic ambition to play for the New York Yankees, the country of Cuba would have experienced a different development this past 50-years. If Adolf Hitler had continued his career as a house painter, today, the whole world would be a different place.

## WRONG DECISIONS BECOME "IF ONLY"

When you make a decision that you later regret, it can become an 'if only' that will stick in your mind forever. This is not a good thing, and it is not necessary, because the alternative outcome may not have been at all the wonderful experience you imagine.

You gave up ballet lessons or ice-skating and now, every time you watch it on television the 'if only' thoughts creep into your mind. Soon, these thoughts can become an obsession, because if you let them continue they can grow out of control. You can become bitter and morose as you worry about the life and career you never had, because of a decision made many years ago.

What you have to think about are the good things on the other side of the balance sheet, all the happiness you have enjoyed because of the decision you made. Your partner in life, your house, career, and your family; these are present today because of your earlier decisions. So what if your horse does came second, you are only one number out in the lottery, and the person you choose to live with is not the 'dream-boat' you first imagined. Get real, and get with it, because nothing and nobody is ideal.

Furthermore, if you watch TV or read the magazines and internet stories, the vast majority of big-money winners find their lives are ruined. Moreover, the majority of people who divorce on a whim, or look for a younger or richer partner, mostly end up thinking 'if only,' because they learn the 'grass is not greener' on the other side.

## IS THERE A BAD DECISION?

The answer is an emphatic "Yes!" There is only one bad decision, and that is indecision. Many people suffer the inability to reach a decision; they procrastinate, and often let the current situation drift along for years while they ponder.

You must become decisive, when it is necessary to make a decision: in both small and great matters, because generally indecision is a sign of the weak. When confronted with the dinner menu in restaurant, your partner will not be impressed if you cannot decide what you want to eat and drink.

Many people say that the only wrong decision is no decision; so when you weigh up in your mind the pros and cons of a situation, do not hesitate, but make your selection boldly and confidently. However, do not make a hasty decision that you may later regret.

A hasty decision is not necessarily a quick decision, but one made without assessing all the factors. Make sure that you know all that is necessary to know, and then make your decision based upon the facts, and the effect they will have in the future.

# Chapter 4

## HOW TO MAKE A RIGHT DECISION

You must make decisions throughout every day; but with many of them, you can make an automatic response. When somebody asks you if you want a cup of tea or coffee, you do not have to ponder the question before making your decision.

When it comes to making a purchase of that invaluable piece of software, eBook, or new lipstick from Paris, you have to weigh up all the factors in your mind; sometimes you have to do this very quickly, or you can miss an opportunity. On the balance sheet, you place such things as the financial cost, the time it will consume, the quality of the product, the reputation of the supplier, the benefits it will provide, the life of the product, and its long-term effects.

You put the plus points on the right-hand side, and the negative ones to the left; and try to score them. Allocation of the points can be made in various ways, and perhaps the best is to make them a percentage. The cost of an item can be a percentage of your weekly expendable income, and if it is something that is going to consume 50% of your free time that week, you put that on the left-hand side. Similarly, where some software is going to save you time, you can work out its percentage and add that to the right-hand column.

This is a time-consuming exercise that can only give you a mathematical answer, but the reason for doing it is that it makes you think about each factor and its real worth in your life. Very often, you will realize that your desire for a particular product is just that-a desire for something new-and it will soon end up in the storage cupboard, which is already full.

Sometimes, however, there are benefits to you and your family that cannot be accurately measured; and a mountain holiday in a rented recreational vehicle that brings your family together can be invaluable, and has to be considered.

## DO YOU LISTEN TO YOUR HEART OR YOUR HEAD?

The problem with looking at a decision logically is that it ignores what your heart is telling you, and you can easily make the wrong choice. You can spend a long time considering all the facts logically and reaching an adult, balanced decision; however, sometimes you arrange the facts to suit the decision you heart wished you take.

All the facts point towards selling your old, roomy family home that requires a lot of repairs and maintenance for that spacious home in the new development; but your heart is telling you that you love the house, location, and neighbors, so you stay.

Your friends gradually move away, your roof leaks, the kids have too far to travel to school, and you get a letter from the council about the new highway that wants part of your backyard! Do not let your emotions sway you into making a decision.

# Chapter 5

## 17 STEPS TO MAKING THE RIGHT DECISION 100% OF THE TIME

Regardless of what religion you are in, it is vital to base your decision on a higher power. It gives you a sense of well-being and pride. Belief on a higher power makes your entire being worthwhile and makes you appreciate life itself.

### Step 1: LEAVE EVERYTHING TO GOD OR A HIGHER POWER

There are things in this life that we have to let be —may it God or whatever we believe as a higher power. Letting things unfold and flow can make you create solid decisions in the long run. Too much expectations lead to greater frustrations. Too much control can't be too good either. Sometimes in life, we must learn to let go. This is what most people call faith. It is the virtue of trusting God or a higher being to control or guide you in life.

## STEP 2: STUDY THE FURTHER WORD OF GOD OR THE LESSONS OF YOUR RELIGION.

This is another way of letting you make the right decision. By guiding yourself based on the wisdom of your ancestors, you'll basically have a moral compass on hand. With this, you'll never be lost especially when it comes to decision making. Sound decisions will become like water to you that flows freely.

## STEP 3: BE WITH PEOPLE WHO KNOW WHERE THEY ARE HEADING

They say when you immerse yourself with a certain culture for a while; it won't be long until you become one of them. By surrounding yourself with wise people who know how to make the right decisions in life, soon enough you'll know the ways of how to make sound decision in life too. Notice how these kinds of people live simple lives? Not much technology, just a simple diet, simple clothing, housing, less property, less money, but still living a content and fulfilled life. Try to discover how they do it, and it might just work for you.

## STEP 4: STAND UP FOR THE TRUTH

In right decision making, never give up. Believe what you know is true and stand up for it. Form solid principles in life which you can use as springboards in making sound decisions. With that, you'll never get lost and confused in formulating life-altering decisions. If ever your decision fails, still stand up for it because you believe it might be good for you. But be humble enough to accept your faults too.

## STEP 5: IS YOUR DECISION BENEFICIAL FOR OTHERS TOO?

Don't be too selfish. Think of how others would benefit from your decision. If your decision would benefit you personally more than any other person, then you might want to re-think it. This is a vital step in right decision making.

## STEP 6: OUR FOUNDING FATHERS HAD TO MAKE SOME VERY DIFFICULT DECISIONS AND ONE OF THE TOOLS THEY USED IS NOW CALLED THE BEN FRANKLIN DECISION MATRIX

Take a piece of paper, get a pen, and draw a horizontal line down the middle of the page, top to bottom. Now on the left top of one column write the word 'Positive', and on the right hand side of the page write the word 'Negative." Make a list of both the pros and cons of your contemplated decision.

I think you see where I am going here. Most of the time, you will immediately see which side of the decision matrix has the most weight or benefit. Sounds simple enough, but if you actually do it, you will be quite amazed...and writing things down also clears your mind which also allows for better decision making. It's science...not just a bunch of words.

Follow these steps, and you will NEVER go wrong Zig Ziglar Says "Successful people don't make the 'right decision'....they make a decision, and then they make it right." If you follow the steps above, you can be confident that your every decision will be one you can make into the right decision, no matter where it leads.

I understand that these steps appear to be fairly cut and dry, but how many of you have actually used them, and/or use them today? It is back to basics my friends...and they will never fail you.

## STEP 7: EXERCISE

You can do any kind of exercise from a walk to going bowling. The purpose behind this is that the body releases specific chemicals into your system when you exercise, and the brain loves the nourishment, and has a positive effect on your overall being. Thrust me and just go for it.

## STEP 8: DO NOT MAKE ANY MAJOR DECISION FOR AT LEAST ON FULL DAY

The brain is such a unique instrument that when we are in the process of making a decision, our subconscious really goes to work...it's incredible really. The biggest key here is sleep on it, an absolute must.

## STEP 9: TALK IT OVER WITH YOUR CLOSE FRIENDS AND/OR FAMILY MEMBERS

Just vent to them, if nothing else (but make sure you don't go into "blaming mode" or it will be counter-productive. Talking out loud can often inspire you with deeper insight, and sometimes you just may get some sound advice.

## STEP 10: PRAY ABOUT IT

Hmm, not a praying person? Then meditate. Not into that either eh? Quiet time perhaps? You get the point. You need time alone when you can detach from your thoughts...get out somewhere and just breathe.

The purpose is just to unwind and let your thoughts flow, without necessarily following any one. Prayer is excellent if you do it in the proper context. You can do meditation, Yoga, Tai Chi...all that is great stuff. Even sitting alone in an ultra-quiet room and/or environment will work wonders and allow the mind to deliver surprising solutions.

## STEP 11: SAY IT OUT LOUD SIMPLY SAY IT TO YOURSELF-OUT LOUD

Does it sound like a good decision? Do you have a good gut feeling about the decision you are about to make? This is a quick easy way to gauge and tap into your intuition and innate intelligence. As I'm sure you have experienced throughout your life, often times it is your initial instinct that was correct-and you either could have saved some time, or made the right decision if you only would have listened to yourself. Essentially, saying it out loud is a different method of asking yourself for approval relative to the decision at hand.

## STEP 12: DO A LITLE RESEARCH WHEN IT COMES TIME TO MAKE THAT IMPORTANT DECISION

Be an expert. Understand the process. Know the limitations and possibilities of everything you do. Remember that there is at least a second side to everything. Therefore, researching and learning everything you can leading up to the actual decision can prove to be very valuable. In doing so, you're setting yourself to make the right decision with high confidence because you understand the dynamics of your decision's consequences based on your insight gained through some simple, quick internet research.

## STEP 13: VISUALIZE THE OUTCOME IN YOUR MIND, WALK YOURSELF THROUGH ACTING OUT ACTUALLY MAKING A DECISION

What do you see happening? How will you react? How will others react? Employing this approach in essence mentally prepares you. Envisioning different scenarios sparks your creativity relative to your situation or decision-and allows you to dive deeper. See yourself making the right decision-or see you becoming successful at the task at hand. This immediately sets the tone and sets you up for a desirable outcome. Learning to visualize can be very powerful and beneficial.

## STEP 14: COME TO TERMS WITH YOUR SITUATION

I realize that coming to terms with a bad situation that happened in your past can be very difficult, especially if you have been through terrible things in life. But whatever occurs in your past will always be the past, it's something that's gone and never to return. Only the memory of yesterday is left.

What's important is to get your life on order, and not become a negative person because of what happened in the past. It serves you no purpose to dwell on things that you cannot change or bring back. It is useless and wasted energy. Your focus should be on moving forward and making the right decision from this point on.

## STEP 15: TRAIN THE MIND

Training the mind is a process, a method of controlling or influencing the way the mind thinks. When you train, you start from small and gradually increase as you go. In other words, adopt habituation, which means to do something until you get accustomed to doing it. Reality says that it takes about 21 days for a habit to take effect. Thus, you need to repeat it over and over again until it becomes a natural flow.

## STEP 16: MAKE THE RIGHT DECISION ALMOST ALL THE TIME

By learning and applying persuasive techniques you will know the same information and techniques that some of the most powerful people in our society have used, people such as Gandhi, Napoleon and Columbus were the leaders of revolutionary change in their respective countries against odds most people thought to be impossible. These people practiced and perfected their techniques that helped them make the correct decisions against grim odds. By learning and applying these techniques you can learn to command attention, get people by your side and be persuasive enough to get anyone to do anything for you without hurting their feelings.

## STEP 17: BECOME A HUMAN LIE DETECTOR

People communicate to you every day and sometimes you may feel they are lying to you, yet you are not exactly sure, I know this has happened to me before, and calling them out would only lead to confrontation, however, by studying persuasive techniques you realize that over 70% of communication is nonverbal. By becoming a body language expert and knowing what signs to look for you when you are being laid to, you can quickly find out such things as who your real friends are, which romantic interest is really into you.

By learning persuasive techniques you can learn how to make the right decisions all the time, know what drives people to make the decisions they do, and learn to make better decisions when purchasing products since you know the same techniques the marketers use to get you to buy their product.

# Chapter 6

# HOW TO COMMIT AND MAKE THE RIGHT DECISIONS

Do you stand immobile at a fork in your career road? Do you feel ambiguous about your job, relationship or purpose? Here are some helpful tips to find the right path to solid psychological ground.

## COMMIT TO YOURSELF FIRST

Commitment to yourself means that you work hardest for your dreams and goals, not everyone else's. Do you feel powerless? You are powerful. The power to change is already in you. Your accomplishments reflect your commitment because even with some bad luck along the way, committed people can become president, or famous, or happy. You can rarely attain big goals without commitment as a top value. Commitment means that if you decide to lose five pounds or fifty, you do not take a few walks then give up. Instead, you work up to a walk of an hour or two each day until you succeed. Commitment means that your finish the projects. Commitment means you show up. Whatever it takes, you are committed. Commitment starts in the morning, and runs until you fall asleep. A nasty failure-voice that says you deserve a break or a treat is not your friend. Commitment bears the pain, and deserves the win of growth.

## THIS IS YOUR DOING

Where you are today is a result of your patterns and past choices. Repeat often, "I gladly take responsibility for changing my life." If you blame someone else, the world, your partner, or God because you are not happy, then you will remain absolutely glued to your excuses and blaming. To get control of your own life means you stop whining and blaming others. If you want things to be different, then you make the choice to be the one to do it. Other people are busy with their own lives. They will walk right over you, and not even notice that you were waiting for someone to make you happy, to fix your pain or to balance your checkbook. What is the point of a lame attitude that is mostly concerned with looking innocent? "I didn't do it." Would you want those words to be a synopsis of an entire irresponsible life? After today, eagerly say, "I did it!" Regarding your life decisions.

## WHO DO YOU WANT TO BE?

Sometimes societal pressures push you into desperately settling for any job or relationship just to fulfill the role. Loss of self-esteem is just one of the severe consequences resulting from succumbing to predetermined societal roles or familial roles. What do you value about your life? List your goals and values in a hierarchy of what is the most important. When you become rock solid with your values then pervasive change happens. Did you include your health near the top? Without your health, you will not have much time to work on your other values and goals. As you take baby-steps in the direction of your "self," expect a backlash of resistance from family and friends who may try to keep you neatly placed as the "old you." That is because they are afraid of change.

## FEEL THE FORCE

You are more than just an individual; you have history! Your DNA goes back to the first people on earth. You have a connection with all the people who have ever lived and strived from the beginning of human history. You can add self-esteem by the ton to whatever you have accomplished in your own life if you think of yourself as a link in a wonderful chain. Remember the people who have died to win us our freedom from old enemies that we now call our friends, from prejudice, chauvinism, religious intolerance, serfdom, slavery-and the list goes on back through history. You come from a long line of people who made good enough decision to survive and reproduce. Pretend the heroes and heroines of yesterday are watching. Just imagine if all history is watching. A good decision gene is in you somewhere.

## PERSONAL GOALS AND VALUES

Do you only "follow directions", or do you "think for yourself?" The personal goals and values you choose are the road signs of every decision you make. What you do is a part of the whole can affect many other lives. Make sure the voice in your head is your own and that your decisions are not just what you were "told" by someone else. List your personal goals and values, and really think them through. Your health, your family's health, your children as a priority, your job as a priority, love, peace of mind, safety, clean world, food, and water, honesty, integrity, sacrificing now for the a peaceful secure future, God, and country-all are possible directions and values to incorporate in your plan.

Think of each of these virtues in the big picture, from a global perspective right down to your own neighborhood and your life. What relationship do you want our world leaders to have with each other-a healthy assertive balanced relationship or an abusive aggressive hate-creating one?

## STAND UP

If you just lie there like a doormat, everyone will walk all over you. That is your fault for lying down on the floor and letting them. The stronger, more aggressive person will trudge right over you to get what they want. Until the weaker person becomes stronger, to the point of balance and equity, his or her business, and personal relationships are horribly unbalanced and eventually fail. Will the strong-willed partner notice the inequity of the relationship and help the weaker one? No. Whatever is different about your beliefs, you can voice your opinion and have a "say." Because each time you do, the prison door opens a little more for oppressed people everywhere.

## TAKE THE HURTS

Take your hits like a winner, admit that you blew it, make the best of a situation or leave it, then continue to whistle while you work. No one wants to come near a big baby, much less take the time to assist you in achieving your personal goals if you just sit there complaining. Choose to take responsibility for you, stand up, move forward, and clean up any mess yourself.

## THERE IS ROOM AT THE TOP

Greed spawns much abuse around the world. You can be someone better than that. Helping others succeed will build your success, and is far more rewarding than trampling people on your way to the top. Take your posse with you and share the wealth and credit. Ask yourself if your plans impinge on anyone else in a way that he or she can no longer be free. You cannot predict how or when your small act of kindness, compassion or courage might change the world or land you a promotion.

## KEEP IT REAL

Without integrity in both public and private actions, the direction you take will have little to do with a positive outcome. Can you raise your self-esteem and stand for more by selecting different values? When you incorporate good values that are your preferences, you will be proud of yourself, and so will your associates and family. Right now, you could begin to stand for something great. Real life soap operas have taught us many powerful and important lessons on the absurdity of life, proving the maxim: "You always get caught", and that the first rule of happiness is to: Stop Lying.

## COMMIT FOR THE DURATION

No pain, no gain. The last stretch of your journey may require some reaching. Maybe you do not have complete assurance that you will succeed, but you get out there anyway and pound away at your goal. Eventually, one day, you are there. Significant change in your life is only possible with this kind of commitment. Do you admire people who commit to their goals? If so, then choose to commit to what you want now, and if it is not what you want later, you can change direction again. Feel confident, let go of all the wavering, questioning, and vacillating of indecision, and simply move forward on your path!

# Conclusion

Thank you again for choosing this book!

I hope this book was able to help you to prepare to make the best possible decision you can make.

Do not make a decision if something deep inside is telling you that it is wrong, because that is when you must listen. However, if you have that niggle inside that is telling you not to do it, then it is probably time to listen.

When it is time to make your next decision, make sure you have all the facts, look at the obvious choice, and if your heart is not against you, go for it with power and confidence.

You do know the right thing to do. It might feel scary. It might be the scariest thing you've ever done. But it will feel right inside. You'll feel free. You'll feel light. It might make your life harder in the short run, but in the long run, you'll look back and be glad you were brave. Glad you trusted your own little rule books those talks to no one else but you. The one that tells you what is and what is not OK for you.

Is it safe for you to decide based on this? Yes, every single time. Above all, we should incline to God's understanding and wisdom and he will help guide our lives with utter discretion.

Finally, if you enjoyed this book, would you be kind enough to leave a review for this book on Amazon? It'd be greatly appreciated!

Thank you and good luck!

# Preview Of 'MIDDLE AGE CAREER CHANGE: HOW TO TURN YOUR LIFE PASSION INTO A CAREER'

## Chapter 1

## MIDDLE AGE CAREER CHANGE

Living in a world with the financial system limping along with a high percent unemployment rate, it's not unusual for even the gainfully employed to test free agency and see what else might be available. In a 2009 Salary.com survey, when global financial markets were still plummeting, more than 65 percent of workers said they were actively looking for new jobs.

It's one thing to change jobs, something most people will do more than 10 times between the ages of 18 and 42, but it's quite another to change careers. Making the leap from a field in which you've been trained and have experience to a new one takes careful consideration planning and the right expectations.

This is true of anyone interested in making a change, but what about professionals who have been in the workforce for 20 or 30-plus years? Baby boomers, born between 1946 and 1964, make up 40 percent of the labor force, and shifting gears later in life to focus on new career objectives can be challenging, but also rewarding. Seasoned professionals often have a different perspective than their younger colleagues.

Middle-aged workers usually place more value on nonmonetary benefits, such as less stress, flexible work schedules and personal fulfillment, so when they're able to change careers they can make the jump to areas that are more professionally fulfilling rather than having to worry about how much they earn.

To check out the rest of (MIDDLE AGE CAREER CHANGE: HOW TO TURN YOUR LIFE PASSION INTO A CAREER) go to on Amazon.com

# Check Out My Other Books

Below you'll find some other popular books that are popular on Amazon and Kindle as well.

**INSECURE:  Stop the Insecurity and Learn how to Overcome Jealousy and Build Self-Esteem.**

**LETTING GO:  Learn How to Embrace the Future.**

**A GUIDANCE TO MENTAL TRAINING:  LEARN HOW TO DEVELOP MENTAL RESILIENCE.**

**MINDSET: HOW YOUCAN BECOME POWERFUL AND ACHIEVE SUCCESS ON YOUR TERMS.**

**FAILURE IS NOT AN OPTION: LEARN HOW TO OVERCOME THE FEAR OF FAILING.**

**MINDFULNESS EXERCISES FOR BEGINNERS.**

**BOUNDARIES IN RELATIONSHIPS:** How to develop boundaries in Marriage and Dating.

**POSITIVE AFFIRMATIONS FOR A BETTER LIFE. LET THE MAGIC HAPPEN!**

# BONUS: SUBSCRIBE TO THE FREE BOOK

## Beginners Guide to Yoga & Meditation

"Stressed out? Do You Feel Like The World Is Crashing Down Around You? Want To Take A Vacation That Will Relax Your Mind, Body And Spirit? Well this Easy To Read Step By Step

E-Book Makes It All Possible!"

Instructions on how to join our mailing list, and receive a free copy of "Yoga and Meditation" can be found in any of my Kindle eBooks.

# NOTES

# NOTES

# NOTES

# NOTES

# NOTES

# NOTES

www.ingramcontent.com/pod-product-compliance
Lightning Source LLC
Chambersburg PA
CBHW070522210526
45169CB00027B/1215